Passions

Susan Patterson

Copyright © 2017 Susan Patterson
Grey Publishing
Oregon City, OR

Illustrations by Susan Laird

ISBN: 978-0-9905898-0-8

All rights reserved. No part of this book may be reproduced or transmitted in any form or by any means, electronic or mechanical, including photocopying, recording, or by any information storage and retrieval system, without permission in writing from the copyright owner.

Printed in the USA

Passion is a most suitable subject for poetry.

Dedication

To those groups and individuals who have sown the
seeds of passion in my life, thank you.

Contents

Preface   1

The stories of passion Speak for each of us.

An Admission of My Truth   5
Filling in the Blanks   6
Never Underestimate the Power of a Glance   8
The Start of Something Right   11
Therefore, It Works   13
The Risk of the Heedless   14
Beauty is in the Eye of the Beholder   17
A Singular Kind of Love   19
Every Love is its Own Definition   21
The Art and Skill of Touch   23
Comfort   25

Passion of the heart shines through the whole of the person.

An Answer to Unrequited Love   29
Why Can't it be Love?   31
Taking Leave, You and I   32
In the Early Twenties   34
Even the Strong Become Weak   37
The Open Opportunity   38
Filled by the Cuppa'   41
Your Second Option   43
The Proposition   45
Oh, The Existential Simplicity of Life   47

Passion may bring us pain, but it may bring us healing as well.

From Time to Time There is a Waiting   51
A Practice of Care   52
The Love Affair of Two Strangers on a Train   54

An All Too Common Story of War	56
The Memory is So Clear	58
The Widow	61
For Those Who Are Afraid of Their Dark	62
No Need for Counting	65
On Staying Behind	67
The Good Love Will Be Timeless, The Great Love Will Be Endless	69
Perfect Union	71
A New Law of Physics	73

Passion combined with love brings forth the most wonderful of outcomes.

The Usual Protestations	77
The Flowers Were Daffodils	78
A Change of Direction	80
A Story of Delicacy	82
The Irresistible Accommodating Seduction	84
Be That As It May	87
Ageless Impressions	88
Something Wonderful Upon Which to Ponder	90
Because We Will Not End	93

Passion gives purpose to our lives.

Preface

Some books just seem to write themselves. Such was the case with *Passions*. As I have explained many times, I write what comes to me. Rarely do I sit down with the intention of putting a poem to paper, and most certainly not a poem of passion. It just doesn't work that way.

This book, a collection of poems of love and sensuality, was penned over a period of years. I did not intend nor plan to compose such a collection. However, like most of my individual works, the book emerged on its own, so to speak. There is reality in the verses given to me to write down. The poetry in *Passions* is honest and lusty. It offers both the serious and the humorous. It can speak to everyone on one level or another.

Passions is not necessarily about people I know. The characters in my poems are, for the most part, fictional and universal. You may see yourself or someone you know in some of the poems. If so, I hope that you are pleased and that you smile with the identity.

Susan Patterson

The stories of passion speak for each of us.

An Admission of My Truth

It would be disingenuous of me
To say
You are nothing.

It would be crass
To say
You are unworthy.

I would be stupid
To think that
You are ordinary.

There are so many
Things about which
I am wrong in life.

My understanding of you
And what you are to me
Is not one of them.

Filling in the Blanks

He opened the door
And there she was,
A cleaning lady in disguise—
Or a goddess incognito.

He wasn't sure because
She couldn't speak.
Her life before had
Made her dumb.
Her life after, had not yet
Arrived.

So, in the middle they met.
He, with his door almost closed,
She, with a space to clean and
A place to shine.

It's been awhile.
He trusts now,
Goes into town and greets
The people he passes
On the streets.

She cleans the windows,
Lights the lamps
And makes the bed.

In the early evening, they
Talk about the day.

Never Underestimate
The Power of the Glance

Now here she is with her purse
And her art and her dogs.
She flounces down the street filling
The space around her and
So much more.
She is what everyone wants.

I love her, by golly, I do. But she takes
No visible heed of me,
Even when she knows me so well.
I am like a big bag of cheap nothing to her.
It is an old story, and
I am left behind like
So many other fools.

If she passes by and doesn't look
My way, I will know there is
Still no chance for me.
Now, here she is, strutting
In front of me without
So much as a glance.   She has
Sealed my fate as surely as if
It was locked away with a key.

There she goes and here I sit.

She is a heartless shrew, by God.
But wait,
Do I see something new?
Yes. She is turning ever so slightly,
And looking, right back to me.

There is hope.

The Start of Something Right

He sat down on the floor next to her.
His curly hair was like an old mop
Which had been used too many times.
The scars that he bore did not show,
And his eyes, bright
As the summer's best day,
Teased with sparkle when
He spoke to her.

"What are you reading?" he prompted.
"Why do you care?" she snipped.

That was the start of their play
Together. That was the start
Of days of abandon to avoid
That which others would consider
Eminently urgent.

But wait, wasn't
Sneaking off to make love
Eminently important as well?

Yes, I dare say it was.

Therefore, It Works

She protects him by telling everything
And by telling nothing at the same time.

He bears witness to her injuries
And salves her wounds with silence.

She goes before and clears the way.
He comes along side and picks up pieces.

He supplies the where with all.
She fashions the breadth of beauty.

She has made him safe from the cruel.
He has made her safe from the fools.

The Risk of the Heedless

I had waited for days.
For the time
When we would talk and touch.
I waited with intelligence and sophistication.
Then it was down to hours.

We would be off together for a mid-day meal.
I was eager.
An amorous hour was my intention.

We left, appearing nonchalant.
But he was busy with things to do.
Then it was over,
Our precious time.

We headed back. My disappointment cut.
We climbed up the old stairs to the world
Where we were not known as one.

Following him like a besotted fluff,
I forgot my sophistication and whined
My letdown.
He turned, as all heroes do,
Grabbed and kissed me
Right there on the stairs.

Forbidden love.

He could have had me on the stairs
For all I cared. I was limp as a dishrag.
It's true.
It was
Worth the wait.
But then,
Would it be so again?
The risk was his.

Beauty is in the Eye of the Beholder

We met and came together in the night.
Lovemaking was compelling.
Now voices are hushed.
Movement is tranquil.

Within hours it will be light and
We will be able to see each other
As we really are.
Morning will come, and with it,
The truth.

We will see the long flaxen hair and
The rich full beard.
We will see firm breasts
And flat stomachs.
We will see the strong leg muscles
That run hard miles,
And the arm muscles that carry
The loads of the world.
We will see our engaging smiles
With white teeth surrounded by
Plump red lips that speak the truth
Out of clear, sound minds.

After four score and ten,
We will see each other
As we really are.

A Singular Kind of Love

They were so close
One would think
That at times, their souls
Mingled in each other's bodies.
Their thoughts were often
Intertwined even when their arms,
Were not.

When separated,
Either for a moment
Or for a millennium,
Neither was quite sure
Of the time spent because,
They were never
Truly apart.

Every Love Is Its Own Definition

They were smoking cigarettes and
Drinking Glen Fiddich straight up,
Out in the open on the veranda.
Even though it was dangerous,
They didn't care.
Danger was their choice.

Both belonged to others.
But they met
Openly,
Broadcasting their
Love, unconsciously
Waiting to be found out,
Almost daring to be found out.

Even so, if they were discovered,
Their lives would change dramatically,
If not end entirely.
Safety was their sacrifice.
It was worth it.
Their passion, though
Not sweet, was addictive.
To them, ordinary love
Was the very definition
Of travesty.

The Art and Skill of Touch

It is a dance of sorts,
Not simply a caress, but
Possibly an artful intention
Of pleasure for the other.
Certainly moments of meaning,
Skillfully designed and delivered.

It is the elegance of
A well-placed hand,
Followed by the ecstasy of
A well-planned touch.

Comfort

Rest with me, my Love.
Calm down your mind.
Release your pain.

Rest with me, my Love.
Let go of your hurry.
Undo your cares.

Rest with me, my Dear
Put down your fears,
Begin to heal.
Let me give you a heart of chamomile.

Passion of the heart shines through the whole of the person.

An Answer to Unrequited Love

If your beloved prefers to sleep
Other than in the all-together,

If your darling does not care
For an afternoon delight,

If your dearest cannot
Canoodle with abandon,

If your partner does
Not dance,

Then consider
An alternative—

A paramour
Who does.

Why Can't it be Love?

Could it be that I am simply taken
By your charming ways?

I think about you when I rise in the
Morning and when I lay down at night.
Some would say
I am enamored with you.

I fantasize and have visions
About us being together.
Others would say
I am infatuated with you.

My heart beats quickly
When we are about to meet.
My breath is short.
I count the days until
We will meet again.
Besotted, for sure.

There are the times when
I dream of us making love
For hours. Can it be
That I am obsessed with you?

Surely, it can't be love.

Taking Leave,
You and I

Now let us
Find indulgence
In one anther's person.
Let us wander the
Intimate hills and valleys
Of the soul encasing
Landscapes
We know so well.

We will call sanctuary
In each other's arms
And find refuge
In the embrace.

You will lie still from
The thoughts that tangle.
I will listen to
Your steady breathing.

We will take leave of
The wars of the world
And the cares that bind.

We will forgive and forget
Yesterday,

Make peace
With tomorrow
And take pleasure
In today.

In The Early Twenties

I remember young love.
Bodies smooth and lithe.
Hands shoved down
Each other's trousers,
Searching for the touch of
Skin that is so satisfying,
But when found,
Craves for the
Ever-deeper thrill.

I remember kissing for
Hours, lips parted and
Tongues exploring the
Depths and hollows of
The wet and warm places.

I remember holding one
Another close for that assurance
Of new commitment; and if
Briefly separated,
Never further than a reach
Away.

I remember young love
With its excitement thinking that
We had a secret about which

No one knew. Our love.
Just ours. Under wraps.
So sly were we. So smug.
But, oh, young love,
Everyone knew.

Even the Strong Become Weak

Was it her inviting
Lips opening in
A consummate kiss?

Was it her
Intoxicating breasts,
Lifting in a caress?

Was it her
Responding heart
Pounding through to his?

It was all of those
And more.

Her laughter, her thoughts,
Those clever eyes that
Witnessed his secret strivings,

With all that was against
His foolish resolve,
How could he not but fold?

The Open Opportunity

The dress fell luxuriously down,
Past the knee and
Onto the well rounded calf.
It had buttons
From the bottom to the top.

All was neatly packaged up,
Except one button,
Which lay strategically
Open near the bosom.
For some reason,
It had been forgotten.
Or maybe the button itself
Rebelled against the containment
Of such beauty. We don't know.

Through that single opening
One could catch glimpse of skin.
It was that sight
Of exquisiteness
Which made one want
To become very small,
Careen through the hole
And wander shamelessly
Over the hills and valleys.

And may it always be so,
That we can have
A glimpse of the forbidden
And know
A hint of the sublime.

Filled by the Cuppa'

There are many reasons why we take tea.
But I must say that
Toasting one's object of affection
Must certainly be the most delighting.

A wink, a nod, a smile,
All are appropriate and admirable
Dalliances at tea.

So lift up your cuppa'.
Tilt it slightly toward your target.
Look your love square in the eye,
Raise your brow slightly and
Smile a secret invitation.

Then wait for the knowing
And glowing response
That only you will see.
Then both you and your love will say,
'Oh, what fulfillment comes from tea!'

Your Second Option

My dear sir,
Come dally with me
I will dilly with you.
We will be naughty
We'll not be nice.

But good sir,
If you cannot dally,
Then I will not dilly.
We'll not be naughty
And that will suffice.

The Proposition

If I promise not
To read poetry and
Promise not to whistle,

Would you come and
Have tea with me and
Down upon my thistle?

Oh, The Existential Simplicity of Life

While slogging through the glen,
I met a girl named Gwen.
We snogged a little,
Snoozed a little,
Then went on
Our way
Again.

Passion may bring us pain, but it may bring us healing as well.

From Time to Time There is a Waiting

I knew I loved you
When we first met.
I also knew I had
Loved you before.

But we are busy and
The choice to be
Together is not
Ours to make.

No matter.
There is a patience.
I know we will
Love again, and
In more ways than
I can now count.
In more ways than
This life
Can comprehend.

A Practice of Care

You walked past me through
The door without saying a word.
I knew something was wrong,
But waited. Then, wisely, I went
To find you.

There you were on the bed.
I lay next to you,
Drawing myself near.
Your back against my chest,
Your head on my arm.

Muscles that held you upright
Had given out. Bone weary,
Your body seemed without spirit.

I heard your short breathing.
I felt your heart quicken then
Slow down, then quicken again.

I pulled you close to me and
Breathed steadily and slowly
To deliver calmness into the air.

You could feel me inhale and
Exhale, and took the pace of
My breathing as your own.
Your sigh evidenced my
Effort was appreciated.

I did this, not because I am
Better or stronger than you,
But because it was my turn.

At another time,
It will be
Your turn.

The Love Affair of Two Strangers on a Train

They sat on the train
Together, side by side.
He, in the aisle seat,
Looking straight ahead,
She, gazing out the window.

For three hours neither of them
Talked. But the presence each
Felt from the other was
So powerful and compelling,
That speaking was not
Entirely necessary.

They just kept looking
Elsewhere.
They were in a world
Together of their own,
Even though they had
Never met.

The end of the line was near.
Finally she said something
About the scenery.
He responded with not
Unexpected knowledge.

It was only a few minutes
Of conversation.
Common, useless words that
One could count on fingers.

The train arrived at
Her stop and she departed
With a very cordial adieu.
Names and cards were
Not exchanged.

He felt the opportunity
Of his lifetime left
When she departed
From that train.

An All Too Common Story of War

It was wartime.
Some people knew it,
Others had no idea.

It seemed that the world
Was as divided as far as
The continents.

Girls were taken and sold.
Bombs, strapped to children.
Rape and torture, routine.

They were both in the
War. Fighting was in
Their blood.

They met at a club.
The dancing there was as
Frenzied as the mortars.

There was no reason to think
The two of them would
Come together.
Differences were their signature.

But in wartime, some people
Make up for differences.
The smart ones do anyway.

They were smart. They
Met and married in what
Seemed like a moment.

They knew their lives
Could end
In another moment.

It was wartime.
Each believed
They had to go and

Fight to the death
In order to
Live a new life.

The Memory is So Clear

She saw him in her dream.
He came for her and they met
On a soft country road.
They embraced as
He put his arm around her.

His broad shoulders
Filled out the brown jacket
He was wearing,
And those shoulders
Were very easy to lean upon.

The love she felt
From him was unworldly.
His acceptance of her was
Absolute and complete.
Such unabashed bliss
Was new to her.

There were no words for
The mystical peace,
The palpable happiness
That filled her when
She was with him.

There was little talking,
They had no need.
Ecstatic in their own company,
They walked forward together,
Until she woke.

She so wanted to return
To the dream.
She still does,
Even today.

The Widow

She would feel the pain of her loss
Start in her stomach.
It would take hold of her muscles and
Twist them around, wringing
The strength out of her.

Then the loss would move up
To her chest where it would
Catch her short of breath until
She couldn't release
The stale air inside of her.

It lingered in her throat, the loss,
Then in her face.
Her eyes were the last to try
To manage it.

Blinking down the misery
And the grief back to her gut,
She would consider
Herself in control.
But after awhile, there,
In her stomach, the suffering
Would start in her again.

The loss would never reach her brain.
So the widow never understood it.

For Those Who Are
Afraid of Their Dark

I shall not be frightened
By the night that comes
Before every dawn.

The darkness, which fills
The corners,
Swallows up the
Spaces and reaches
From room to room;

The darkness, which creeps
Along hour by hour
Around the house
And lingers at the door;

That darkness of night
Shall not be the bane
Of my existence.

The veil that protects me
From the unseen evil
And the unclear
Danger, shall not
Be rent in twain.

There is light just around
The corner. Just past the
Window. Just within
My reach.

No Need for Counting

How many shoulders will it
Take for you to stand upon,
Until you can stand
Tall on your own?
How many arms will it
Take to wrap around
Your frame until
You feel safe?
Pairs of eyes to keep guard
As you walk, lest you
Fall into the pit?
What about the hands needed
To reach down and
Pull you out of the pit?
Ears to listen to your cries for help
And to your stories of triumph?
How many pairs of legs will it
Take to walk with you
Until you are able to
Take the steps alone?
And when you are ready,
The heart to let you go?

As many as it takes.

On Staying Behind

You will be with me.
I will not let you go.
No. No, I won't.
Well—
Yes, of course I will.
I would not bind you
To this sodden life.
But in the same time,
In the same word,
In the same spirit,
I will not let you go.
I will see you
In the dishes
That I wash,
In the silver
That I store.
I will hear your
Voice in the sounds of the house,
In the rising up and the lying down.
I will hold you until
We are together
Yet again,
For a longer while
In another space,
At another time.

The Good Love Will Be Timeless, The Great Love Will Be Endless

They wanted and waited
For nothing.
Time was neither a
Friend nor an enemy.
It wasn't really part of their life.

Time belonged to other people,
As did politics
And occupation
And rush.

Theirs was a world of
Tranquility by demand,
Intellect by nature,
Detachment by choice.

Love had found them young
And they claimed it
As their past and future.
There is no doubt,
No fear,
No need for explanation.

And so it will be,
No matter what.

Perfect Union

Their love has the
Energy of new creation
And the immensity old.

It doesn't now,
Nor ever will,
Want for more.

A New Law of Physics

Passion of the heart and
Intelligence of the mind
Exist in equal importance.

One cannot fully live
Without an adequate
And balanced
Supply of each.

Passion combined with love brings forth the most wonderful of outcomes.

The Usual Protestations

'To you my dear.'
A cup of tea is lifted
Out of respect
And in love.

'No, no, no to you!'
A glass of wine
Is raised
In dissent.

They bicker
Back and forth
In mock challenge,
Neither of them
Prevailing in the
Comic dispute.

It doesn't matter
Who is victorious.
Such battles are common,
In their very uncommon life.

The Flowers Were Daffodils

He wanted her to notice him.
He sat day after day on the step
By where she passed,
Wanting so very desperately
To talk with her,
To be with her.
She would not notice him.

He set out with an ingenuous plan.
He gave each person who
Passed by his step, a flower. Every day.
He did not miss a soul.
He gave one to her every day as well.
She did not especially notice him.

Flowers to everyone in hopes of
Engaging someone.
A notable effort, indeed.
But after weeks of
Taking the blossoms,
She still did not pay him heed.

Finally he offered her more than a
Flower. He quietly presented a gift
Of only himself, in the form of
A marriage proposal.

At last she allowed herself
To see him. To see his efforts.
Who could turn away
Such a suitor?
She took the risk and
Accepted his gift,
Right then and there.

Each year,
To commemorate that day,
He and she hand out
Flowers to strangers.

A Change of Direction

He and she were striding along the
Busy street,
Discussing work issues,
As was their matter of course.

Infatuation had enticed
Them earlier that year,
And the two often escaped
And enjoyed lunch together.

Their conversation flowed
Smoothly as they were now
Comfortable with each other.
But something happened that day.

Unexpectedly, he turned to her and
Without a pause between sentences,
Matter-of-factly said,
'It's time we kissed'.
Just like that.
She stopped and readied herself,
Tilting her head towards him.

Their lips, parting slightly, met in
Coordinated perfection.
That was all. It was over.

A breathtaking understatement of
Unrealized intention.
They looked back at the street,
Without saying a word
And went on their way,
About their business.

And he knew. And she knew.
But what they did
Not know,
And were not prepared for,
Was that they had
Turned a corner
Together.

A Story of Delicacy

They met under the covers,
This couple in the night.
He and she barely touched,
But their subtle intensity
Was intoxicating.

With her fingers, she
Followed the lines of his life that
Were etched in his hands.
She spent a half a hour just on the
Right hand alone.
The touch lifted her.

Then she went to his left hand. It
Too told his story.
She felt it in the hollow of his palm
And in the strength of his fingers.
She was reminded of what she
Already knew about him.

Their lips almost met,
Their bodies almost entwined,
But intentionally they did not.
Magnetism ensued.
Hands heeded the passion.
He responded

By placing her hand
Just where it needed to be.
She did the same.

The Irresistible Accommodating Seduction

On Monday he hugged her
From behind as she
Washed the dishes.
She leaned into him and
Felt warm and comfortable.

Tuesday he gently
Touched her shoulder as
He passed her chair.
Later he reached under the table
For her hand and silently
Massaged the delicate palm.

Wednesday he drew her
To him and kissed her mouth.
As she let go of the embrace,
He tenderly pulled her back in
For a more sultry moment.

Thursday morning, he greeted
Her with composed passion.
Before they drifted off to sleep
That night, he whispered
A promise of touching affections
For her to dream upon.

It took almost a week to create
A fervent desire, but one can
Only imagine the
Friday surprise they enjoyed.

Be That As It May

She buttons her shirts wrong,
Or worse yet, she puts them
On inside out and then she is
Still a button or two off.

She wears her shoes on the
Wrong feet and doesn't notice.
Her hair sticks out oddly
And she doesn't seem to mind.

However, she cleans up quite well,
And many people believe her to be
Beautifully elegant all of the time.

He sees her as she truly is,
Whatever that may be,
A goddess or a fool.

Yes, you've got it,
He loves her all the same,
If not all the more.

Ageless Impressions

He wants to remember
What she is like and
How his hand feels on her body.
It has been there countless times before.
The imprint of this ritual
On his mind is deep.

His hand starts at the
Side of her chest,
Slides its way down and
Dips into the waist,
Up at the hip
And down to the thigh.

They call to mind the important,
Forgetting what is hurtful or useless.
Changes in her do not matter
Because he pictures her young.
She knew his strength and sees it still.
Down the side, in at the waist,
Up at the hip and down to the thigh.

She wants to remember what
His hand feels like on her body.
It's been there countless times before.
The imprint is deep in her mind.

Down the side, in the waist,
Up the hip and down the thigh.

Something Wonderful Upon Which to Ponder

We sleep together,
Like spoons, as they say.
Your chest and my back,
Leaning against each other
In perfect match and comfort.
Our hands rest upon each other's
Thighs. Our feet are intertwined.

Ten thousand years from now
I will remember the sense
And the warmth of you.
Twenty thousand years from
Now, I will hear your heart beat
And feel you breathe.

Thousands of ages after that,
Whether we are together
Or not,
I will remember your touch
And feel your warmth
And know your strength.

It will be as if
We were always
As one,

And for that,
I am grateful.

Because We Will Not End

Meet me after awhile
Where the earth meets the sky,
Where flowers rise up to become clouds.
Watch for me where the firmament
Melts and evaporates into the heavens,
Where waters flow into the sun.
I will be there.
Either, before or after you,
I do not know which.

But shall we promise
To look for and to find
Each other,
In the morning,
At the start of a new day,
Where the earth meets the sky?

Passion gives purpose to our lives.

About the Author

Susan Patterson is an author of the heart and writer for the soul. Her work, it has been said, is so sharp, so intricate, that it is like a Faberge egg. Ms. Patterson's audience is worldwide and declares her writing to be in the top caliber of modern poets.

Ms. Patterson has authored two books of tea poetry, *Musings With a Cuppa-The Poetry of Tea* and *Heart to Heart-Considered Sentiments for Teatime*; and one book and a CD of contemporary poetry, *Unnoticed Moments*. Her third book of poetry, Passions, is a collection of love poems. She also has a book of prose memoirs, *Tom and Irma-Memories of the 1950's*.

Susan Patterson has a Bachelor of Arts in English and a Masters in Business Administration. She and her husband, James, live a quiet life in Oregon of the United States. Please visit, www.EarleneGrey.com to schedule appearances and to purchase books.

Made in the USA
Las Vegas, NV
09 July 2024

92085348R00066